MR. BOSTON

summer
COCKTAILS

edited by Anthony Giglio and Jim Meehan
photography by Ben Fink

WILEY

john wiley & sons, inc.

Copyright © 2010 by Barton Incorporated. All rights reserved

Published by John Wiley & Sons, Inc., Hoboken, New Jersey

Published simultaneously in Canada

For general information on our other products and services or for technical support, please contact our Customer Care Department within the United States at (800) 762-2974, outside the United States at (317) 572-3993 or fax (317) 572-4002.

Wiley also publishes its books in a variety of electronic formats. Some content that appears in print may not be available in electronic books. For more information about Wiley products, visit our web site at www.wiley.com.

Library of Congress Cataloging-in-Publication Data

Giglio, Anthony.
Mr. Boston summer cocktails / edited by Anthony Giglio and Jim Meehan ; photography by Ben Fink.
p. cm.
title: Summer cocktails
Includes index.
ISBN 978-0-470-18489-9 (cloth)
1. Cocktails. I. Meehan, Jim. II. Title. III. Title: Summer cocktails.
TX951.G4763 2009
641.8'74--dc22
2009014014

Printed in China

10 9 8 7 6 5 4 3 2 1

contents

welcome!

You are holding in your hands the "Summer Cocktails" edition of the definitive guide to mixing perfect drinks. *Mr. Boston Bartender's Guide* has been the official go-to manual for bartenders and spirits professionals since it was first published in 1935. It has been endorsed, consulted, and considered a basic tool by bartenders for decades. In fact, more than 11 million copies have been in print since it first appeared shortly after the repeal of Prohibition.

This book is the first of its kind for *Mr. Boston*: a guide written specifically with warm weather entertaining in mind. Our decision to focus on these thirst-quenching libations was inspired by the dynamic energy we're seeing bartenders and mixologists pouring into seasonally inspired cocktails, working more like chefs to capture the essence of year-round seasonality. They also understand that as the weather warms up, our tastes, cravings, and even our socializing habits change. We'd like to think that this latest guide from *Mr. Boston* would have very much pleased Leo Cotton, the author of the very hard-to-find first edition of what was then called *Old Mr. Boston De Luxe Official Bartenders Guide*, as he was known to be the life of any party he attended.

And speaking of parties, we've gathered more than 100 recipes for this edition that are guaranteed to please your guests at any summer gathering. We've categorized these recipes into five thematic chapters, each encompassing drinks that range from classics and riffs on classics to cutting edge and totally trendy.

We must admit here that we encountered some interesting ingredients while consulting the most imaginative, inventive, and— yes, we're going to say it—brilliant bartenders in the world, including specialty spices, flavored syrups, and just-plain-funky concoctions (rose petal jam, anyone?). What we found, however, is that any dogged drinks maven can do a quick search on the Internet to find a recipe or retail source for just about anything these bartenders poured for us. Still, it's worth reminding our readers that some of the best cocktails ever created were those employing substitutes plus a little imagination. Consider yourselves inspired.

And speaking of inspiration, if there's one common theme that unites all of these recipes it is the emphasis on ingredients. That's because the star, or point of reference, of every cocktail—the spirit, whether it be gin, brandy, or amaro—is just the beginning. The transformation of these elixirs into something more palatable occurs when you blend them with ingredients containing little or no alcohol to cut their strength. This is where mixology comes into play. While our team of gifted mixologists was charged with the task of creating beautifully balanced cocktails and then writing accurate recipes for them, there's always a little give and take in cocktail craftsmanship akin to how a chef adjusts sauces just before serving. That's your job after replicating these recipes. Before you serve them, taste them for balance. Do they taste too boozy? Perhaps more fresh juice. Too sweet? A dash of bitters should balance that. Too watery? You need fresh ice cubes—the bigger, the better! It's all in your hands.

Before you continue reading, however, please take a moment to think about the responsible use and serving of alcoholic drinks. The consumption of alcohol dates back many millennia, and in many cultures throughout the world, it is part of social rituals associated with significant occasions and celebrations. The majority of adults who choose to drink do not abuse alcohol and are aware that responsible drinking is key to their own enjoyment, health, and safety, as well as that of others, particularly when driving.

Finally, a word on the employment of flower garnishes and fresh egg whites in some of the cocktails in this book. For recipes calling for flower garnishes, only food-safe, edible flowers should be used. These can be found in the herb section of your supermarket and should always be organic and pesticide-free. And while we are thrilled to see the recent rebirth of egg-based cocktails, we understand our readers' concerns about salmonella poisoning associated with raw eggs. While salmonella poisoning from eggs is relatively rare, there are alternatives to using raw eggs if you have any doubts about your eggs. If a recipe calls for raw egg whites, you can use either whites from pasteurized shell eggs (separated from the yolks by hand) or packaged egg whites found in the dairy aisle of the supermarket, which have also already been pasteurized. Hopefully, you'll feel inspired—and safe enough—to make your own frothy summer cocktails with fresh egg whites.

So, congratulations! You're well on your way to creating cocktails that will enhance your summertime entertaining—and make the task of mixing drinks easier. Let's raise a proverbial glass in honor of Mr. Boston as he was introduced in his 1935 debut:

> Sirs—May we now present to you Old Mr. Boston in permanent form. We know you are going to like him. He is a jolly fellow, one of those rare individuals, everlastingly young, a distinct personality and famous throughout the land for his sterling qualities and genuine good fellowship. His friends number in the millions those who are great and those who are near great even as you and I. He is jovial and ever ready to accept the difficult role of "Life of the Party," a sympathetic friend who may be relied upon in any emergency. Follow his advice and there will be many pleasant times in store for you.
>
> Gentlemen, Old Mr. Boston

contributors

Erik Adkins

Colin Appiah

Jeff Berry

Greg Best

Jacques Bezuidenhout

Richard Boccato

Jamie Boudreau

Jacob Briar

Tad Carducci

Kathy Casey

Martin Cate

Brother Cleve

John Coltharp

Jane Danger

Alex Day

Dale DeGroff

John Deragon

Damon Dyer

Daniel Eun

Giuseppe Gonzalez

Kenta Goto

Robert Hess

Francesco LaFranconi

James Lee

Jeffrey Lindenmuth

Ryan Magarian

Vincenzo Marianella

Lynnette Marrero

Mickey McIlroy

Jim Meehan

Junior Merino

Brian Miller

Andy Minchow

Jeffrey Morgenthaler

Jonathan Pogash

Christy Pope

Jonny Raglin

Gary Regan

Julie Reiner

Lydia Reissmueller

Patricia Richards

Armando Rosario

Audrey Saunders

Joseph Schwartz

Willy Shine

Aisha Shorpe

Joaquin Simo

Chad Solomon

Stanislav Vardna

Artemio Vasquez

Thad Vogler

Phil Ward

Neyah White

Damian Windsor

David Wondrich

Naren Young

EQUIPMENT

THE RIGHT TOOLS make mixing drinks easier. Some drinks simply can't be made without them.

BOSTON SHAKER: Two-piece set for shaking cocktails, comprising a mixing glass and a slightly larger metal container that acts as a cover for the mixing glass. The mixing glass can be used alone for stirring drinks that aren't shaken.

BARSPOON: Shallow spoon with a long twisted handle, used for stirring drinks.

HAWTHORN STRAINER: Perforated metal strainer held in place by a wire coil, used with the metal half of a Boston shaker.

JULEP STRAINER: Perforated spoon-shaped strainer used with a mixing glass.

COBBLER SHAKER: Metal pitcher with
a tight-fitting lid, under which sits a
strainer.

STAND BLENDER: Absolutely
necessary to make frozen drinks,
purée fruit, and even crush ice for
certain recipes.

CUTTING BOARD: Wood or plastic,
used when cutting fruit.

PARING OR UTILTY KNIFE: Small
sharp knife used to cut fruit.

MUDDLER: Looks like a wooden pestle, the flat end of which is
used to crush and combine ingredients in a serving glass or
mixing glass.

GRATER: Useful for grating nutmeg and other whole spices.

BOTTLE OPENER: Essential for opening bottles that don't have twist-off caps.

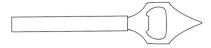

CHURCH KEY: Usually metal; pointed at one end to punch holes in the tops of cans, while the other end is used to open bottles.

CORKSCREW: There are a myriad of styles from which to choose. Professionals use the waiter's corkscrew (which looks like a large penknife), the Screwpull, or the Rabbit corkscrew. The winged corkscrew found in most homes is considered easiest to use but often destroys the cork.

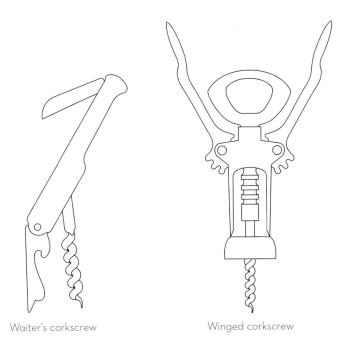

Waiter's corkscrew   Winged corkscrew

CITRUS REAMER OR JUICER: Essential for juicing fruit; comes in several styles. The strainer bowl-style has a pointed cone built in and a spout for pouring. There is also the wooden handle-style with the cone attached, which must be used with a strainer to remove pulp. Another style resembles two nested ice cream scoops and allows juice to be squeezed with one hand.

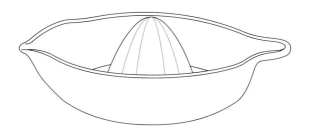

JIGGER: Essential for precise measuring; typically has two cone-shaped metal cups conjoined at the narrow ends, each side representing a quantity of ounces (quarter, half, whole, etc.), marked in fractions by lines etched in the metal.

ICE BUCKET WITH SCOOP AND TONGS: A bar without ice is like a car without gas. Use the scoop—never the glass—to gather ice to put in a mixing glass or shaker, and tongs to add individual cubes to a prepared drink.

MISCELLANEOUS ACCOUTREMENTS: Sipsticks or stirrers, straws, cocktail napkins, coasters, and cocktail picks.

GLASSWARE

CLEAN, POLISHED GLASSES show off good drinks to great advantage. The best glasses should be thin-lipped and transparent and sound off in high registers when "pinged." These glasses can be used to make most of the mixed drinks and cocktails found in this book:

COCKTAIL GLASS (also known as martini glass): Typically 5 to 7 oz., but sometimes much larger.

COLLINS GLASS: Tall and narrow, typically 12 to 14 oz.

HIGHBALL GLASS: Shorter Collins glass, typically 8 to 10 oz.

OLD-FASHIONED GLASS: Wide and squat, typically 12 to 14 oz.

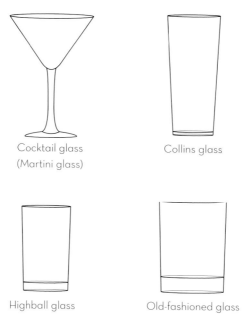

Cocktail glass
(Martini glass)

Collins glass

Highball glass

Old-fashioned glass

CHAMPAGNE COUPE: Cocktail glass with rounded curves and flat bottom, typically 5 to 8 oz.

CHAMPAGNE FLUTE: Long stem with a test tube–like bowl to preserve the bubbles, typically 6 to 8 oz.

HURRICANE GLASS: Short stem, hourglass shape, typically 16 to 20 oz.

RED-WINE GLASS: Stem glass with large, round, or tulip-shape bowl, typically 8 to 12 oz., though sizes vary widely.

WHITE-WINE GLASS: Stem glass with tulip-shape bowl, typically 8 to 12 oz., though sizes vary widely.

Champagne coupe   Champagne flute   Hurricane glass

Red-wine glass   White-wine glass

TECHNIQUES

Chilling Glassware

Always chill before you fill—even your cocktail shaker before mixing the drink. There are two ways to make cocktail glasses cold:

1. Put the glasses in the refrigerator or freezer an hour before using them.

2. Fill the glasses with ice and water, then discard when drink is ready.

Choosing Fruit and Fruit Juices

Whenever possible, use only *fresh* fruit. Wash the outside peel before using. Fruit can be cut in wedges or slices. If slices are used, they should be cut about 1/2 inch thick and slit toward the center to fix the slice on the rim of the glass. Cucumbers are typically cut into 1/2-inch-thick slices. Wedges are typically made by cutting citrus fruit in half longitudinally, then in thirds, forming six equal parts. Make sure garnishes are fresh and cold.

When mixing drinks containing fruit juices, always pour the liquor last. Squeeze and strain fruit juices just before using to ensure freshness and good taste. Avoid artificial or concentrated substitutes.

When recipes call for a twist of lemon peel, rub it around the rim of the glass to deposit the oil on it. Twist the peel skin side down so that the oil drops into the drink, then drop in the peel skin side up. The lemon oil is an ingredient in the drink and gives added character to the cocktail.

Muddling Fruits and Herbs

Muddling is a simple mashing technique for pressing the oil out of fruit and herbs such as mint in the bottom of a glass. You can buy a wooden muddler in a bar supply store. Muddlers typically range from six to ten inches long, flattened on one end (the muddling end) and rounded on the other (the handle). When muddling pulpy or fibrous fruit, you might want to double strain the liquid through a tea strainer before serving the drink.

Opening Champagne or Sparkling Wine

When the bottle is well chilled, wrap it in a clean towel. Remove the foil capsule and undo the wire around the cork, holding the cork down with one hand while loosening the wire with the other—never letting go of the cork. Pointing the bottle away from people and priceless objects, grasp the bottle by the indentation on the bottom and, leveraging the pressure between both hands, slowly turn the bottle (not the cork!) until the cork comes free. Pour slowly down the center of the glass.

Opening Still Wine

Cut the capsule neatly around the neck with a sharp knife just below the top. Peel off, exposing the cork. Wipe off the cork and bottle lip. Insert the corkscrew and turn until the corkscrew is completely inside the cork. With a steady pull, remove the cork. If the cork crumbles or breaks, pour the wine through a small fine-mesh strainer into another container for serving. The host or hostess should taste the wine to check its quality before offering it to guests.

Rimming a Glass

This technique separates the pros from the amateurs. Into a saucer or a small bowl pour kosher salt—never use iodized table salt—sugar, or spices, depending on the drink. Using a wedge of fresh lemon or lime, carefully wet only the outside rim of the cocktail glass. Holding the glass sideways, dab the rim into the salt while slowly turning the glass, until the entire rim is covered. Finally, hold the glass over the sink and tap the glass gently against your free hand to knock off any excess salt. The effect is a delicately salted rim that looks almost frosted. You can also rim half the glass to give your guests the option to enjoy the drink with or without extra seasoning or sugar.

Rolling Drinks

To prevent drinks that call for thick juices or fruit purées from foaming, roll them instead of shaking. Rolling is the act of pouring the drink—a Bloody Mary, for example—back and forth between two shaker glasses. After rolling the drink a half dozen times, it should be completely mixed and ready to be strained.

Shaking

As a rule of thumb, shake any drink made with juices, eggs, or cream.

ASSEMBLING

Assemble the ingredients in the mixing glass part of the Boston shaker, adding the fresh juice first, then the dashes, modifiers, and the base spirit, and ending with the ice.

SEALING

Place the metal half of the Boston shaker over the mixing glass sitting on the bar. Holding the glass firmly, clap the upturned flat end of the metal half twice with the heel of your free hand to form a seal. To test the seal, slightly lift the whole shaker off the bar by the metal top to see if it holds; if not, seal it again or replace one of the parts.

FLIPPING, THEN SHAKING

Turn the conjoined shaker over so that the mixing glass is on top and the metal half rests on the bar. Grasp the shaker with the metal half sitting securely in the palm of one hand and the other hand wrapped securely over the upturned end of the mixing glass. Shake hard with the glass on top. (In case the seal breaks, the liquid will stay in the bigger metal half.) Shake vigorously, rendering the drink effervescent.

BREAKING IT UP

After shaking, set the shaker on the bar, glass-side down. Then, clasp one hand around the equator of the conjoined shaker and, using the heel of your other hand, hit the top rim of the metal shaker bluntly to break the seal. If it doesn't work the first time, rotate the shaker slightly and try again.

STRAINING AND POURING

If you're the least bit theatrical, this is the time for it. Just remember: Always use the Hawthorn strainer (springform) with the metal part of the set, and the julep strainer (holes) with the mixing glass. (See Straining at right.)

Stirring

While you can prepare stirred drinks like Negronis, Martinis, and Manhattans in any number of vessels, the glass part of the Boston shaker is considered best. After you've assembled your liquids and ice, hold the barspoon by the shaft between your thumb and first two fingers. Plunge the spoon end into the mixing glass and begin twirling the spoon back and forth between your fingers, while at the same time moving the spoon around in the glass. Do this for at least 10 seconds to completely chill the cocktail, and also provide sufficient dilution.

Straining

STRAINING FROM THE METAL HALF OF THE SHAKER

Place the Hawthorn strainer securely on top, then put your forefinger and middle finger on top of the strainer while grabbing the shaker with your thumb, ring, and pinky fingers. Hold the shaker tightly and pour slowly at first to prevent the drink from splashing out of the glass. When straining into a cocktail glass, pour the liquid into the center of the glass to help avoid spillage. As the pour slows toward the last ounce, draw your hand up high over the middle of the cocktail glass, emptying the last of the liquid with a snap of the shaker.

STRAINING FROM A MIXING GLASS

Place the julep strainer over the top of the glass with the concave side facing up. Grab the glass toward the top with your thumb and three fingers, and then curl your forefinger over the handle of the strainer, holding it firmly in place. Strain following the directions above.

HOW MANY DRINKS PER BOTTLE?

Cocktails, Mixed Drinks

1.5-OUNCE LIQUOR SERVINGS

BOTTLES	1	2	4	6	8	10	12
750-ML	16	33	67	101	135	169	203
1.5-LITER	39	78	157	236	315	394	473

Fresh
DIRECT

We feel the effort it takes to incorporate seasonal fresh fruits in our cocktails is justly rewarded within seconds of the very first taste of the cocktail bearing—literally—the fruits of our labor. Whether you're simply muddling fresh mint with limes or painstakingly pitting cherries to mash into simple syrup, the results always far outweigh the task, imbuing your drinks with flavor and intensity that can only come from fresh, unprocessed fruit. The following recipes feature, for the most part, fruits that we're more likely to find during the warmer months at farm stands brimming with berries, melons, and vegetables—though thanks to global shipping, you might be able to find many of these ingredients year-round. However, as we strive to become ever more conscious of the purity and freshness of the ingredients in our cocktails, we'd like to suggest at least trying to procure ingredients grown locally if possible.

Blackbeard Punch

4 FRESH BLACKBERRIES
1/2 OZ. AGAVE NECTAR
1 OZ. FRESH PINEAPPLE JUICE
1/2 OZ. FRESH LEMON JUICE
3/4 OZ. AQUAVIT
1 1/2 OZ. GIN
GARNISH: MINT SPRIG

In a mixing glass muddle the blackberries. Add the rest of the ingredients, cover, and shake without ice. Pour the contents into the center of an old-fashioned glass filled with crushed ice so the blackberries form a mound at the top of the glass. Garnish with the mint sprig.

Brazilian Raspberry Rickey

4 FRESH RASPBERRIES
3/4 OZ. SIMPLE SYRUP
1 OZ. FRESH LIME JUICE
2 OZ. CACHAÇA
SODA WATER

In a mixing glass muddle the raspberries with the simple syrup. Add the lime juice and cachaça, top with ice cubes, cover, and shake thoroughly. Strain into a chilled highball glass and top with soda water.

Brazilian Raspberry Rickey

Cherry Pop

Cherry Caipirinha

½ LIME, QUARTERED

4 FRESH BING CHERRIES, PITTED

½ OZ. SIMPLE SYRUP

½ OZ. FALERNUM

2 OZ. CACHAÇA

In a mixing glass muddle the lime and cherries with the simple syrup. Add the falernum and cachaça, top with ice cubes, cover, and shake thoroughly. Pour the entire contents of the shaker into a chilled old-fashioned glass.

Cherry Pop

4 FRESH BING CHERRIES, PITTED

½ OZ. SIMPLE SYRUP

¾ OZ. FRESH LEMON JUICE

¼ OZ. MARASCHINO LIQUEUR

2 OZ. GIN

GARNISH: FRESH BING CHERRY, ON THE STEM

In a mixing glass muddle the pitted cherries with the simple syrup. Add the rest of the ingredients, top with ice cubes, cover, and shake thoroughly. Strain into an old-fashioned glass filled with crushed ice and garnish with the bing cherry on the stem.

Company B

1 FRESH STRAWBERRY, HULLED

1/2 OZ. FRESH LEMON JUICE

1/4 OZ. AGAVE NECTAR

1/2 OZ. CAMPARI

1/2 OZ. TRIPLE SEC

1 1/2 OZ. BLANCO TEQUILA

GARNISH: STRAWBERRY SLICE

In a mixing glass muddle the strawberry. Add the rest of the ingredients, top with ice cubes, cover, and shake thoroughly. Strain into a chilled cocktail glass and garnish with the strawberry slice.

Cucumber-Cantaloupe Sour

3/4 OZ. FRESH LEMON JUICE

2 OZ. FRESH CANTALOUPE JUICE

1/2 OZ. HONEY SYRUP (SEE PAGE 36)

1 1/2 OZ. GIN

GARNISH: CUCUMBER SLICE

Combine all of the ingredients in a cocktail shaker. Add ice cubes, cover, and shake thoroughly. Strain into a chilled cocktail glass and garnish with the cucumber slice.

Cucumber-Cantaloupe Sour

Dulce de Fresa

2 FRESH STRAWBERRIES, HULLED

1 TSP. AGAVE NECTAR

¾ OZ. FRESH LEMON JUICE

¼ OZ. ALLSPICE LIQUEUR

2 OZ. REPOSADO TEQUILA

GARNISH: LEMON TWIST

In a mixing glass muddle the strawberries with the agave nectar. Add the rest of the ingredients, top with ice cubes, cover, and shake thoroughly. Strain into an old-fashioned glass filled with ice cubes and garnish with the lemon twist.

tradesecret

Go to the farmers' market or grocery store before deciding which drinks to serve that night. Chances are, the peaches or strawberries you hoped to use in a drink may not be ripe, but another fruit will catch your eye. Most of the fruit you buy at the grocery store has been bred to look pleasing, so make sure to use your senses of touch and smell to ensure that the flavor will follow through in your drink.

Georgia Mule

1 PEACH SLICE, PEELED, PLUS 1 FOR GARNISH

1/2 OZ. FRESH LEMON JUICE

2 DASHES OF PEACH BITTERS

1 1/2 OZ. VODKA

1 1/2 OZ. GINGER BEER

Muddle 1 peach slice in a Collins glass. Fill the glass with ice cubes. Build the other ingredients, in order, stir thoroughly, and garnish with the remaining peach slice.

Kingpin Fruit Cup

1 LEMON WEDGE

1 LIME WEDGE

3 1/2" CUCUMBER SLICES, PLUS 1 FOR GARNISH

5 FRESH RASPBERRIES

1/2 OZ. SIMPLE SYRUP

1/2 OZ. TRIPLE SEC

1/2 OZ. SWEET VERMOUTH

2 OZ. VODKA

SODA WATER

In a mixing glass muddle the lemon and lime wedges, 3 cucumber slices, and the raspberries with the simple syrup. Add the triple sec, vermouth, and vodka, top with ice cubes, cover, and shake thoroughly. Strain into a Collins glass filled with ice cubes, top with soda water, and garnish with the remaining cucumber slice.

Madrono Cobbler

1 FRESH STRAWBERRY, HULLED

1/2 OZ. DEMERARA SYRUP (SIMPLE SYRUP MADE WITH DEMERARA SUGAR)

1 PINCH OF GROUND CINNAMON

1/2 OZ. AMER PICON

3 OZ. DRY SACK SHERRY

GARNISH: CINNAMON STICK

In a mixing glass muddle the strawberry with the Demerara syrup. Add the rest of the ingredients, top with ice cubes, cover, and shake thoroughly. Strain into a highball glass filled with crushed ice and garnish with the cinnamon stick.

Market Street Julep

3 1" FRESH PINEAPPLE CUBES

6 MINT LEAVES

1/2 OZ. SIMPLE SYRUP

2 OZ. PISCO

GARNISH: 2 MINT SPRIGS

In a julep cup muddle the pineapple cubes and mint leaves with the simple syrup. Add the pisco and fill the glass with crushed ice. Swizzle until the cup frosts, then garnish with the mint sprigs.

Market Street Julep

Melon Stand

Marylebone

3 FRESH BLACKBERRIES

¾ OZ. SIMPLE SYRUP

¾ OZ. FRESH LEMON JUICE

¼ OZ. ALLSPICE LIQUEUR

2 OZ. GIN

In a mixing glass muddle the blackberries with the simple syrup. Add the rest of the ingredients, top with ice cubes, cover, and shake thoroughly. Strain through a fine-mesh sieve into a chilled cocktail glass.

Melon Stand

4 1" WATERMELON CUBES

¾ OZ. FRESH LEMON JUICE

½ OZ. SIMPLE SYRUP

½ OZ. APEROL

2 OZ. GIN

GARNISH: WATERMELON BALL

In a mixing glass muddle the watermelon cubes. Add the rest of the ingredients, top with ice cubes, cover, and shake thoroughly. Strain into a Collins glass filled with crushed ice and garnish with the watermelon ball.

Muddled Mission

1 FRESH STRAWBERRY, HULLED
¾ OZ. FRESH LEMON JUICE
½ OZ. ELDERFLOWER LIQUEUR
¼ OZ. YELLOW CHARTREUSE
1½ OZ. GIN

In a mixing glass muddle the strawberry. Add the rest of the ingredients, top with ice cubes, cover, and shake thoroughly. Strain into a chilled cocktail glass.

Plum Fairy Cobbler

1 FRESH PLUM HALF, PITTED
2 DASHES OF ORANGE BITTERS
½ OZ. TRIPLE SEC
½ OZ. ABSINTHE
3 OZ. SAUVIGNON BLANC
GARNISH: PLUM SLICE

In a mixing glass muddle the plum half. Add the rest of the ingredients, top with ice cubes, cover, and shake thoroughly. Strain into a highball glass filled with crushed ice. Garnish with the plum slice.

The Ramble

4 FRESH RASPBERRIES

1 OZ. FRESH LEMON JUICE

¾ OZ. SIMPLE SYRUP

2 OZ. GIN

In a mixing glass muddle the raspberries. Add the rest of the ingredients and shake thoroughly without ice. Pour the contents into the center of a Collins glass filled with crushed ice so the raspberries form a mound at the top of the glass.

tradesecret

When a fruit used to make one of your favorite drinks goes out of season, high-quality preserves or marmalade are among the best substitutes for the real thing. Fruit juices and nectars from concentrate are commonly loaded with sugar and preservatives, which heavily compromise the integrity of a cocktail. In the days before refrigeration, families stocked their pantries with home-preserved fruit from the harvest. Try substituting preserves and marmalade—and if you like the results, why not try making them yourself? They're easy!

The Red Coat

3 FRESH BING CHERRIES, PITTED
1/2 OZ. SIMPLE SYRUP
1 EGG WHITE
1 OZ. SAUVIGNON BLANC
2 OZ. GIN

In a mixing glass muddle the cherries with the simple syrup. Add the rest of the ingredients, cover, and shake without ice. Add ice cubes, cover, and shake again. Strain into a chilled cocktail glass.

Tequila Smash

4 FRESH BLUEBERRIES
4 FRESH BING CHERRIES, PITTED
1/2 OZ. FRESH LIME JUICE
1/2 OZ. MARASCHINO LIQUEUR
2 OZ. BLANCO TEQUILA
GARNISH: LIME WHEEL, FRESH CHERRY, PITTED, AND LARGE FRESH BLUEBERRY

In a mixing glass muddle the blueberries and 4 cherries. Add the rest of the ingredients, top with ice cubes, cover, and shake thoroughly. Strain into an old-fashioned glass filled with ice cubes and garnish with the lime wheel skewered with the cherry and the blueberry.

Thoroughbred Cocktail

Thoroughbred Cocktail

1¹/₂ OZ. FRESH PEACH PURÉE

1 OZ. FRESH LEMON JUICE

3 DASHES OF ANGOSTURA BITTERS

2 OZ. BOURBON WHISKEY

SODA WATER

GARNISH: FRESH PEACH SLICE

Build in a Collins glass filled with crushed ice, top with soda water, and swizzle until the glass frosts. Garnish with the peach slice.

The Water Maker

4 1" WATERMELON CUBES
3/4 OZ. FRESH LEMON JUICE
3/4 OZ. SIMPLE SYRUP
1 1/2 OZ. BOURBON WHISKEY
GARNISH: LEMON TWIST

In a mixing glass muddle the watermelon cubes. Add the rest of the ingredients, top with ice cubes, cover, and shake thoroughly. Strain into an old-fashioned glass filled with crushed ice and garnish with the lemon twist.

AND GOOD FOR YOU, *Too!*

Science appears to have reached a consensus. Alcohol, the stuff found in wine, beer, and spirits, has clear health benefits when consumed in moderation, lowering the risk of heart disease and improving overall cardiovascular health. Most doctors will tell you it's no reason to start drinking, but if you keep it to about two drinks per day for men and one for women, there appears little reason to deprive yourself of the visceral pleasure of a well-made drink. These selected recipes add fresh and healthful ingredients to the mix, whether tomatoes containing the antioxidant lycopene or vitamin C–packed citrus. The notion isn't totally new: Gin was conceived as a medicine, and many of the most famous liqueurs, such as Chartreuse, were created as herb-infused panaceas. We can't guarantee the recipes will do anything more than yield a well-balanced, tasty drink, but even skeptics must agree: This is good medicine for the soul.

After Burner

1 DILL SPRIG

2 ½" CUCUMBER SLICES, PLUS 1 FOR GARNISH

¾ OZ. SIMPLE SYRUP

¾ OZ. FRESH LIME JUICE

2 OZ. GIN

In a mixing glass muddle the dill and 2 cucumber slices with the simple syrup. Add the lime juice and gin, top with ice cubes, cover, and shake thoroughly. Strain through a fine-mesh sieve into a chilled cocktail glass and garnish with the remaining cucumber slice.

Amante Picante

2 ½" CUCUMBER SLICES, PLUS 1 FOR GARNISH

2 CILANTRO SPRIGS

1 OZ. FRESH LIME JUICE

2 DASHES OF GREEN (JALAPEÑO) TABASCO SAUCE

1 OZ. SIMPLE SYRUP

2 OZ. BLANCO TEQUILA

In a mixing glass muddle 2 cucumber slices and the cilantro. Add the rest of the ingredients, top with ice cubes, cover, and shake thoroughly. Strain into a chilled cocktail glass and garnish with the remaining cucumber slice.

After Burner

Angkor Wat

Angkor Wat

1 SERRANO CHILE SLICE, SEEDED

8 FRESH CILANTRO LEAVES

3/4 OZ. SIMPLE SYRUP

3/4 OZ. FRESH LIME JUICE

2 OZ. COCONUT RUM

GARNISH: LIME WHEEL OR CILANTRO SPRIG

In a mixing glass muddle the chile and cilantro with the simple syrup. Add the lime juice and rum, top with ice cubes, cover, and shake thoroughly. Strain into a chilled cocktail glass and garnish with the lime wheel or cilantro.

Azteca

3 FRESH SAGE LEAVES, PLUS 1 FOR GARNISH

1/2 OZ. SIMPLE SYRUP

3/4 OZ. FRESH LIME JUICE

1/2 OZ. YELLOW CHARTREUSE

1/2 OZ. ELDERFLOWER LIQUEUR

2 OZ. BLANCO TEQUILA

In a mixing glass muddle 3 sage leaves with the simple syrup. Add the rest of the ingredients, top with ice cubes, cover, and shake thoroughly. Strain through a fine-mesh sieve into a chilled cocktail glass and garnish with the remaining sage leaf.

Capri Cooler

5 FRESH BASIL LEAVES

1/2 OZ. SIMPLE SYRUP

3/4 OZ. FRESH LEMON JUICE

1/2 OZ. LIMONCELLO

11/2 OZ. CITRUS VODKA

GINGER BEER

GARNISH: LEMON WHEEL

In a mixing glass muddle the basil leaves with the simple syrup. Add the lemon juice, limoncello, and vodka, top with ice, cover, and shake thoroughly. Strain through a fine-mesh sieve into a Collins glass filled with ice cubes, top with ginger beer, and garnish with the lemon wheel.

Carter Beats the Devil

1 OZ. FRESH LIME JUICE

PINCH OF GROUND CHILE

1/2 OZ. AGAVE NECTAR

1/4 OZ. MEZCAL

11/2 OZ. REPOSADO TEQUILA

GARNISH: LIME WHEEL

In a mixing glass combine all of the ingredients, top with ice cubes, cover, and shake thoroughly. Strain into a chilled cocktail glass and garnish with the lime wheel.

Capri Cooler

The Dastardly Deed

4 FRESH BASIL LEAVES, PLUS 1 FOR GARNISH

3/4 OZ. SIMPLE SYRUP

3/4 OZ. FRESH LIME JUICE

2 OZ. VODKA

In a mixing glass muddle 4 basil leaves with the simple syrup. Add the lime juice and vodka, top with ice cubes, cover, and shake thoroughly. Strain into a chilled cocktail glass and garnish with the remaining basil leaf.

tradesecret

When muddling herbs and spices, it's crucial to release their aromatic oils: The idea is to *press*, not to pulverize. Chris Gallagher's Pug Muddler, available directly from the maker himself (jcgallagher08@hotmail.com) and David Nepove's Mr. Mojito Muddler (www.mrmojito.com) are perfect for the job. Pouring the finished drink through a fine-mesh sieve into the glass is a nice touch: That way you can enjoy the flavor without getting tiny leaves or seeds stuck between your teeth.

Far East Side

1 FRESH SHISO LEAF, PLUS 1 FOR GARNISH

3/4 OZ. ELDERFLOWER LIQUEUR

1/4 OZ. FRESH LEMON JUICE

1/2 OZ. BLANCO TEQUILA

2 OZ. JUNMAI SAKE

In a mixing glass muddle 1 shiso leaf with the elderflower liqueur. Add the rest of the ingredients, top with ice cubes, cover, and shake thoroughly. Strain through a fine-mesh sieve into a chilled cocktail glass and garnish with the remaining shiso leaf.

Kiwi & French

2 KIWI SLICES, PEELED

1/2 OZ. SIMPLE SYRUP

1/2 OZ. GREEN MELON LIQUEUR

3/4 OZ. FRESH LEMON JUICE

1 EGG WHITE

1 1/2 OZ. GIN

1 OZ. CHAMPAGNE

GARNISH: LEMON TWIST

In a mixing glass muddle the kiwi and simple syrup. Add the rest of the ingredients and shake without ice. Add ice cubes, cover, and shake thoroughly. Strain into a chilled Champagne coupe and top with Champagne. Garnish with the lemon twist.

Mediterranean Breeze

1 THYME SPRIG, PLUS 1 FOR GARNISH

2 LEMON WEDGES

3/4 OZ. LIME JUICE

1 OZ. LIMONCELLO

1 1/2 OZ. CITRUS VODKA

In a mixing glass muddle 1 thyme sprig and the lemon wedges with the lime juice. Add the limoncello and vodka, top with ice cubes, cover, and shake thoroughly. Strain into a chilled cocktail glass and garnish with the remaining thyme sprig.

Pernelle

1 ROSEMARY SPRIG, PLUS 1 FOR GARNISH

1/2 OZ. SIMPLE SYRUP

1 OZ. FRESH LEMON JUICE

1/2 OZ. PEAR BRANDY

1/2 OZ. ELDERFLOWER LIQUEUR

2 OZ. VODKA

SODA WATER

In a mixing glass muddle 1 rosemary sprig with the simple syrup. Add the lemon juice, brandy, liqueur, and vodka, top with ice cubes, cover, and shake thoroughly. Strain into a chilled highball glass filled with ice cubes, top with soda water, and garnish with the remaining rosemary sprig.

Pernelle

Piña Margarita

Piña Margarita

5 1" FRESH PINEAPPLE CUBES
5 FRESH CILANTRO LEAVES
1/2 OZ. AGAVE NECTAR
3/4 OZ. FRESH LIME JUICE
1 1/2 OZ. BLANCO TEQUILA
GARNISH: CILANTRO SPRIG

In a mixing glass muddle the pineapple cubes and cilantro leaves with the agave nectar. Add the lime juice and tequila, top with ice cubes, cover, and shake thoroughly. Strain into an old-fashioned glass filled with ice cubes and garnish with the cilantro sprig.

Pink Elephant

3/4 OZ. FRESH GRAPEFRUIT JUICE
1/2 OZ. FRESH LIME JUICE
1/4 OZ. SIMPLE SYRUP
1/4 OZ. CRÈME DE MÛRE
1/4 OZ. MARASCHINO LIQUEUR
2 OZ. GIN

Combine all of the ingredients in a cocktail shaker, add ice cubes, cover, and shake thoroughly. Strain into a chilled Champagne coupe.

Rosarita

1 ROSEMARY SPRIG, PLUS 1 FOR GARNISH

1/2 OZ. SIMPLE SYRUP

3/4 OZ. FRESH LIME JUICE

1/4 OZ. TRIPLE SEC

1 1/2 OZ. BLANCO TEQUILA

In a mixing glass muddle 1 rosemary sprig with the simple syrup. Add the rest of the ingredients, top with ice cubes, cover, and shake thoroughly. Strain into a chilled cocktail glass and garnish with the remaining rosemary sprig.

Rude Sage Cosmo

3 FRESH SAGE LEAVES, PLUS 1 FOR GARNISH

3/4 OZ. TRIPLE SEC

1 OZ. WHITE CRANBERRY JUICE

1/2 OZ. FRESH LIME JUICE

2 OZ. BLANCO TEQUILA

In a mixing glass muddle 3 sage leaves with the triple sec. Add the rest of the ingredients, top with ice cubes, cover, and shake thoroughly. Strain into a chilled cocktail glass and garnish with the remaining sage leaf.

Shiso No Natsu

4 FRESH SHISO LEAVES, PLUS 1 FOR GARNISH
½ OZ. DRY VERMOUTH
1 OZ. GIN
1½ OZ. JUNMAI SAKE

In a mixing glass muddle 4 shiso leaves. Add the rest of the ingredients, top with ice cubes, and stir thoroughly. Strain through a fine-mesh sieve into a chilled cocktail glass and garnish with the remaining shiso leaf.

Stoli Noir

3 FRESH BLACKBERRIES
1 ROSEMARY SPRIG
1/2 OZ. AGAVE NECTAR
3/4 OZ. FRESH LIME JUICE
2 OZ. BLACKBERRY VODKA
GARNISH: LEMON TWIST

In a mixing glass muddle the blackberries and rosemary with the agave nectar. Add the lime juice and vodka, top with ice cubes, cover, and shake thoroughly. Strain through a fine-mesh sieve into a chilled cocktail glass and garnish with the lemon twist.

tradesecret

Try matching your modifiers with your base spirit. If the drink calls for tequila, use agave nectar in place of cane-based sugar, the natural choice for rum-based cocktails. The same goes for liqueurs: grape-based curaçaos such as Grand Marnier pair beautifully with Cognac, while grain- or beet-based liqueurs such as Cointreau mix seamlessly with gins and vodka. Nose your chosen base spirit and use the flavors as a hint: herbal tones can be accentuated by vermouth or fresh herbs, honeyed notes by substituting honey syrup (equal parts honey and hot water; stir until dissolved) for simple syrup, or spice with a couple dashes of aromatic bitters.

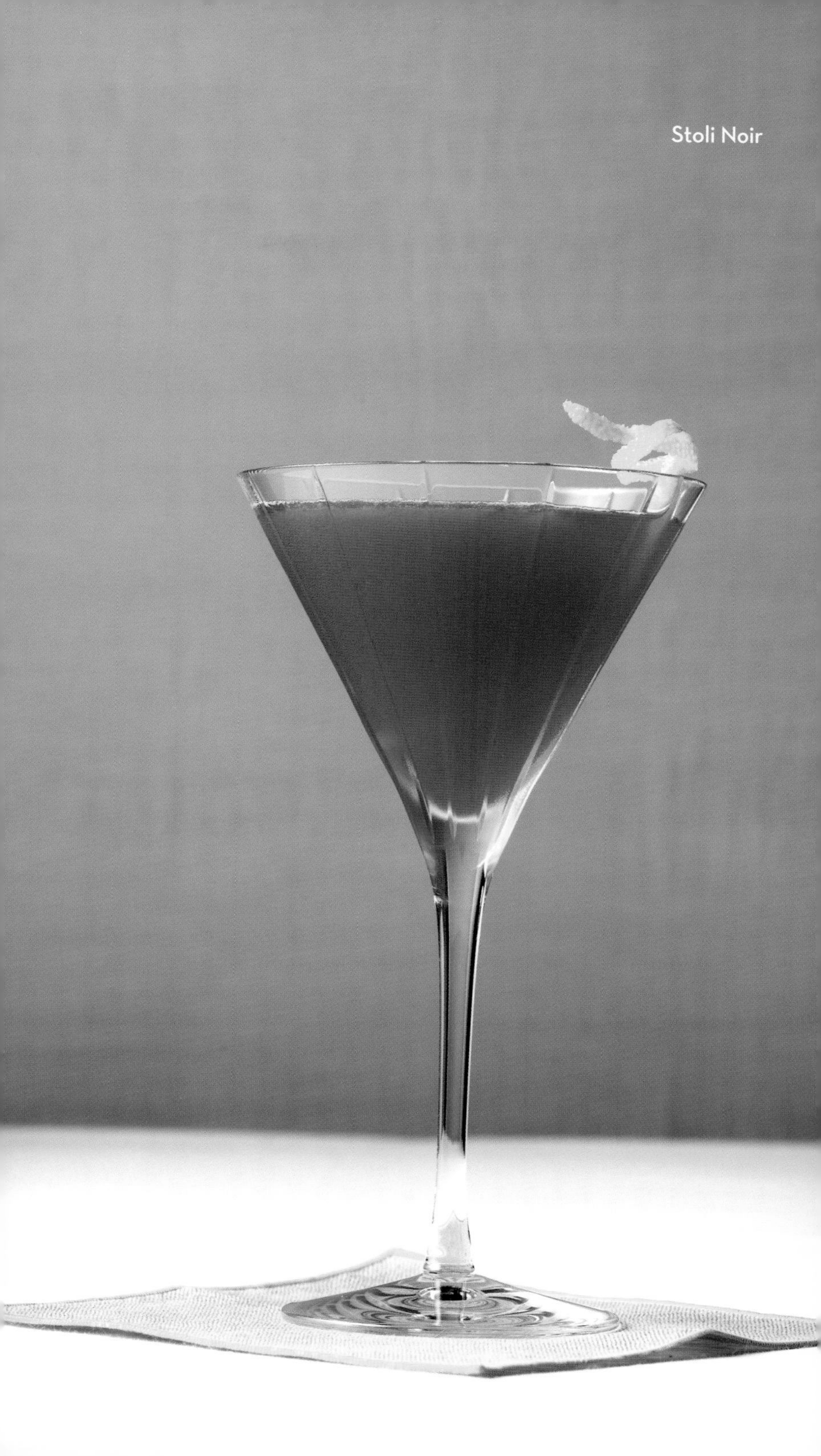

Stoli Noir

Tomato Daiquiri

Tiger Tanaka

1 1/4" PIECE PEELED FRESH GINGER

3 FRESH CILANTRO LEAVES

3/4 OZ. PINEAPPLE JUICE

1/2 OZ. LIMONCELLO

2 OZ. CITRUS VODKA

In a mixing glass muddle the ginger and cilantro. Add the rest of the ingredients, top with ice cubes, cover, and shake thoroughly. Strain into a chilled cocktail glass.

Tomato Daiquiri

3 FRESH CHERRY TOMATOES

1 OZ. FRESH LIME JUICE

1 DASH OF ANGOSTURA BITTERS

1 OZ. SIMPLE SYRUP

2 OZ. AGED RUM

In a mixing glass muddle the tomatoes. Add the rest of the ingredients, top with ice cubes, cover, and shake thoroughly. Strain into a chilled daiquiri glass.

Vanderbilt Avenue Martini

1 FRESH SAGE LEAF, PLUS 1 FOR GARNISH
1/2 OZ. ELDERFLOWER LIQUEUR
3/4 OZ. FRESH PINEAPPLE JUICE
1 OZ. CUCUMBER VODKA
TO RIM GLASS: 1 LEMON WEDGE, SUGAR

In a mixing glass muddle 1 sage leaf with the elderflower liqueur. Add the pineapple juice and vodka, top with ice cubes, cover, and shake thoroughly. Rim a chilled cocktail glass with lemon wedge and sugar. Strain into the cocktail glass and garnish with the remaining sage leaf.

Wise Old Sage

4 FRESH SAGE LEAVES, PLUS 1 FOR GARNISH
1/2 OZ. AGAVE NECTAR
11/2 OZ. FRESH GRAPEFRUIT JUICE
1/2 OZ. ORANGE CURAÇAO
11/2 OZ. WHITE RHUM AGRICOLE

In a mixing glass muddle 4 sage leaves with the agave nectar. Add the rest of the ingredients, top with ice cubes, cover, and shake thoroughly. Strain into a chilled cocktail glass and garnish with the remaining sage leaf.

tradesecret

Reserve less-than-perfect-looking herbs for muddling and use the best-looking ones for garnish. For mint, pick off the bottom leaves and store the sprigs stem down in a glass filled with ice water. Cutting skin-on cucumbers into 1/2-inch slices gives you the best balance between the heart's floral, melon flavors and the peel's herbal, bitter flavors. It's best to wear gloves when seeding hot peppers.

W.Y.B.M.A.D.I.I.T.Y.?

4 FRESH STRAWBERRIES, PLUS 1, STEM-ON, FOR GARNISH

3 FRESH KAFFIR LIME LEAVES, PLUS 1 FOR GARNISH

2 TBSP. BROWN SUGAR

3/4 OZ. FRESH LIME JUICE

1/2 OZ. PUNT E MES

2 OZ. VANILLA VODKA

In a mixing glass muddle 4 hulled strawberries and 3 lime leaves with the brown sugar. Add the rest of the ingredients, top with ice cubes, cover, and shake thoroughly. Strain into an old-fashioned glass filled with ice cubes and garnish with the remaining strawberry and lime leaf.

Before, DURING, AND AFTER

Is there a wrong occasion for a cocktail? We'd like to think not, provided you know how to choose the right cocktail for the occasion. Most liqueurs, both bitter and sweet, were developed as digestives to soothe the stomach and aid digestion after an enjoyable meal. Taken alone, some of the most famous, such as Campari or Fernet Branca—or even cocktail bitters—bear a striking resemblance to face-twisting childhood medicines. When mixed, however, these ingredients balance beautifully with spirits, juices, and sweeteners to add unmatched complexity to our drinks. No longer just for after dinner, dry, bracing, and pleasingly bitter drinks are ideal to stimulate the appetite. And by incorporating sparkling wine and food ingredients, cocktails can even give wine a run for its money at the dinner table. If none of these conditions exist, we may break out the shaker regardless. Sometimes, you see, a well-crafted cocktail is the occasion.

Air Mail

½ OZ. FRESH LIME JUICE
½ OZ. HONEY SYRUP (SEE PAGE 36)
1 OZ. WHITE RUM
CHAMPAGNE

Combine the first three ingredients in a cocktail shaker, add ice cubes, cover, and shake thoroughly. Strain into a chilled Champagne coupe and top with Champagne.

Arch Angel

1 ½" CUCUMBER SLICE
¾ OZ. APEROL
2¼ OZ. GIN
GARNISH: LEMON TWIST

In a mixing glass muddle the cucumber slice. Add the Aperol and gin, top with ice cubes, and stir thoroughly. Strain into a chilled cocktail glass and garnish with the lemon twist.

Blood Orange

1½ OZ. FRESH ORANGE JUICE

¾ OZ. CAMPARI

¾ OZ. DRY VERMOUTH

1½ OZ. GIN

Combine all of the ingredients in a cocktail shaker, add ice cubes, cover, and shake thoroughly. Strain into a chilled Champagne coupe.

tradesecret

Champagne is the world's most celebrated sparkling wine and works wonders in cocktails, but it comes with a steep price. When budget constraints demand that you substitute, let the ingredients in the drink you're making be your guide. For drinks made with white spirits and citrus, look for aromatic sparkling wines such as prosecco, Crémant d'Alsace, or riesling *sekt* brut from Austria. When a cocktail is made with bitters, vermouth, or bittersweet liqueurs such as Campari, substitute yeasty, full-bodied sparkling wines such as cava, Franciacorta, or Vouvray. Spending a little time learning about lesser-known wines will pay off when you're stocking your refrigerator.

Botticelli

1¹/₂ OZ. FRESH GRAPEFRUIT JUICE

¹/₂ OZ. HONEY SYRUP (SEE PAGE 36)

³/₄ OZ. APEROL

1¹/₂ OZ. VODKA

PROSECCO

GARNISH: GRAPEFRUIT TWIST

Combine the first four ingredients in a cocktail shaker, add ice cubes, cover, and shake thoroughly. Strain into a chilled Champagne coupe, top with prosecco, and garnish with the grapefruit twist.

Bubbles and Strawberries

3 FRESH STRAWBERRIES, HULLED

¹/₂ OZ. FRESH LEMON JUICE

³/₄ OZ. SIMPLE SYRUP

1 PINCH OF FRESHLY CRACKED BLACK PEPPER

1¹/₂ OZ. CITRON VODKA

CHAMPAGNE

GARNISH: FRESH STRAWBERRY SLICE

In a mixing glass muddle the strawberries with the lemon juice and simple syrup. Add the pepper and vodka, top with ice cubes, cover, and shake thoroughly. Strain into a chilled Champagne coupe, top with Champagne, and garnish with the strawberry slice.

Botticelli

Casino Royale

Casino Royale

1 OZ. FRESH ORANGE JUICE

¼ OZ. FRESH LEMON JUICE

½ OZ. MARASCHINO LIQUEUR

1 OZ. GIN

CHAMPAGNE

GARNISH: ORANGE TWIST (OPTIONAL)

Combine the first four ingredients in a cocktail shaker, add ice cubes, cover, and shake thoroughly. Strain into a chilled Champagne coupe, top with Champagne, and garnish with the orange twist, if using.

Corpse Reviver No. 2

¾ OZ. FRESH LEMON JUICE

¾ OZ. COINTREAU

¾ OZ. LILLET BLANC

¾ OZ. GIN

1 DASH OF ABSINTHE

Combine the first four ingredients in a cocktail shaker, add ice cubes, cover, and shake thoroughly. Strain into an absinthe-rinsed chilled cocktail glass.

Electric Ladyland

½ OZ. FRESH LIME JUICE

1 TSP. ROSE JAM (AVAILABLE AT SPECIALTY RETAILERS AND ONLINE; SUBSTITUTE RASPBERRY JAM IF DESIRED)

1½ OZ. PISCO

CHAMPAGNE

GARNISH: EDIBLE ROSE PETAL

Combine the first three ingredients in a cocktail shaker, add ice cubes, cover, and shake thoroughly. Strain into a chilled Champagne coupe, top with Champagne, and garnish with the rose petal.

Imperial Basil Mimosa

Imperial Basil Mimosa

6 FRESH BASIL LEAVES

¼ OZ. SIMPLE SYRUP

2 OZ. FRESH ORANGE JUICE

1 DASH OF ANGOSTURA BITTERS

1 OZ. VODKA

CHAMPAGNE

GARNISH: BASIL SPRIG

In a mixing glass muddle the basil leaves with the simple syrup. Add the next three ingredients, top with ice cubes, cover, and shake thoroughly. Strain into a chilled Champagne flute, top with Champagne, and garnish with the basil sprig.

La Fleur de Paradis

½ OZ. FRESH LEMON JUICE
½ OZ. FRESH GRAPEFRUIT JUICE
2 DASHES OF ORANGE BITTERS
¼ OZ. SIMPLE SYRUP
¾ OZ. ELDERFLOWER LIQUEUR
2 OZ. GIN
CHAMPAGNE
GARNISH: EDIBLE PANSY

Combine the first six ingredients in a cocktail shaker, add ice cubes, and shake thoroughly. Strain into a chilled Champagne coupe, top with Champagne, and garnish with the edible pansy.

La Perla

1½ OZ. REPOSADO TEQUILA
1½ OZ. MANZANILLA SHERRY
¾ OZ. PEAR LIQUEUR
GARNISH: LEMON TWIST

Add all of the ingredients to a mixing glass, then add ice cubes. Stir thoroughly and strain into a chilled cocktail glass. Garnish with the lemon twist.

The Old Cuban

4 FRESH MINT LEAVES

1 OZ. SIMPLE SYRUP

¾ OZ. FRESH LIME JUICE

2 DASHES OF ANGOSTURA BITTERS

1½ OZ. AGED RUM

CHAMPAGNE

In a mixing glass muddle the mint leaves with the simple syrup. Add the next three ingredients, top with ice cubes, cover, and shake thoroughly. Strain into a chilled Champagne coupe and top with Champagne.

Plummed Away

1½ OZ. APPLE JUICE

½ OZ. FRESH LEMON JUICE

½ OZ. SIMPLE SYRUP

¾ OZ. PLUM WINE

¾ OZ. IRISH WHISKEY

GARNISHES: LEMON TWIST, BASIL LEAF (OPTIONAL)

Build in a highball glass filled with ice cubes. Stir, then garnish with a lemon twist and a basil leaf, if using.

Polanka

4 FRESH MINT LEAVES

1/2 OZ. ELDERFLOWER LIQUEUR

1/2 OZ. FRESH LIME JUICE

1/2 OZ. APPLE JUICE

1 OZ. BISON GRASS VODKA

CHAMPAGNE

GARNISH: APPLE SLICE

In a mixing glass muddle the mint leaves with the elderflower liqueur. Add the next three ingredients, top with ice cubes, cover, and shake thoroughly. Strain into a chilled Champagne flute, top with Champagne, and garnish with the apple slice.

Positano

1 FRESH STRAWBERRY, HULLED

1/2 OZ. SIMPLE SYRUP

1/2 OZ. FRESH LEMON JUICE

1/2 OZ. CAMPARI

1 OZ. GIN

CHAMPAGNE

GARNISH: BRANDIED CHERRY, ON THE STEM

In a mixing glass muddle the strawberry with the simple syrup. Add the next three ingredients, top with ice cubes, cover, and shake thoroughly. Strain into a chilled Champagne flute, top with Champagne, and garnish with the brandied cherry.

Primavera

4 FRESH BASIL LEAVES, PLUS 1 FOR GARNISH

3/4 OZ. SIMPLE SYRUP

3/4 OZ. FRESH LIME JUICE

1 EGG WHITE

1/2 OZ. ABSINTHE

2 OZ. GIN

SODA WATER

In a mixing glass muddle 4 basil leaves and the simple syrup. Add the next four ingredients, cover, and shake without ice. Add ice cubes and shake again. Strain into a chilled highball glass filled with ice cubes, top with soda water, and garnish with the remaining basil leaf.

tradesecret

Apértif cocktails are meant to whet your appetite by getting your digestive juices flowing. The low proof and higher acidity of these drinks tend to make them highly quaffable. Whenever you serve drinks, and especially apértifs, make sure to serve food as well. If you're feeling adventurous, serve something that shares ingredients with the drinks, such as ceviche or fresh salsa. Otherwise, bite-size snacks that can be served without silverware are perfect when your guests are engaged in conversation with a cocktail in hand and don't want to bother with a knife and fork.

Rossa Italiano

Rossa Italiano

¾ OZ. FRESH LEMON JUICE

¾ OZ. GIN

¾ OZ. PUNT E MES

¾ OZ. APEROL

GARNISH: LEMON TWIST

Combine all of the ingredients in a cocktail shaker, add ice cubes, cover, and shake thoroughly. Strain into a chilled highball and garnish with the lemon twist.

Trident

2 DASHES OF PEACH BITTERS

½ OZ. CYNAR

1 OZ. AQUAVIT

1 OZ. MANZANILLA SHERRY

GARNISH: LEMON TWIST

In a mixing glass combine all of the ingredients, top with ice cubes, and stir thoroughly. Strain into a chilled cocktail glass and garnish with the lemon twist.

Woolworth

2 OZ. BLENDED SCOTCH WHISKY

1 OZ. MANZANILLA SHERRY

½ OZ. BÉNÉDICTINE

2 DASHES OF ORANGE BITTERS

GARNISH: LEMON TWIST

Combine all of the ingredients in a mixing glass, then add ice cubes. Stir thoroughly and strain into a chilled Champagne coupe. Garnish with the lemon twist.

Tall, DARK, AND TROPICAL

Many people like to pose the hypothetical question, Were we stranded on a desert island with ingredients to fill our shaker but once, which would be our only cocktail of choice? It's a nightmare scenario that makes us shudder. But after careful consideration, we've narrowed it down to the ones in this chapter, guided by the premise that Mr. Boston never sails without a well-stocked bar. All these drinks taste of the tropics, bursting with pineapple, allspice, cinnamon, and that most equatorial of spirits, rum. At the same time, they evoke the civilized world. They like to be seen poolside, singing along with the band in a voice of clinking ice and sporting their own personal umbrellas to shield them from the sun. For warm weather entertaining, choosing to serve any one of these refreshing long drinks will transport your party to an island paradise. Fortunately, however, you don't have to choose just one.

Ancient Mariner

Ancient Mariner

¾ OZ. FRESH LIME JUICE

½ OZ. FRESH GRAPEFRUIT JUICE

½ OZ. SIMPLE SYRUP

¼ OZ. ALLSPICE LIQUEUR

1 OZ. AGED RUM

1 OZ. DARK RUM

GARNISHES: LIME WEDGE, MINT SPRIG

Combine all of the ingredients in a cocktail shaker, add ice cubes, cover, and shake thoroughly. Strain into an old-fashioned glass filled with ice cubes and garnish with the lime wedge and mint sprig.

Castaway

3 OZ. FRESH PINEAPPLE JUICE

3/4 OZ. COFFEE LIQUEUR

1 1/2 OZ. AGED RUM

GARNISHES: MARASCHINO CHERRY, FRESH PINEAPPLE WEDGE

Combine all of the ingredients in a cocktail shaker, add ice cubes, cover, and shake thoroughly. Strain into a hurricane glass filled with crushed ice and garnish with the cherry skewered into the pineapple wedge.

Center City Swizzle

3/4 OZ. FRESH LEMON JUICE

3/4 OZ. GINGER SYRUP

1/4 OZ. VELVET FALERNUM

1 OZ. AMONTILLADO SHERRY

1 OZ. STRAIGHT RYE WHISKEY

GARNISHES: ANGOSTURA BITTERS, MINT SPRIG

Build in a pilsner glass, then top with crushed ice. Swizzle and top with more ice. Garnish with 2 dashes of Angostura bitters and the mint sprig.

Cuzco

Coconut Caipirinha

1/2 LIME, HALVED (2 QUARTERS)
3/4 OZ. SIMPLE SYRUP
1/2 OZ. UNSWEETENED COCONUT WATER
2 OZ. CACHAÇA
GARNISH: BASIL SPRIG

In a mixing glass muddle the lime quarters with the simple syrup. Add the coconut water and cachaça, top with ice cubes, cover, and shake thoroughly. Strain into an old-fashioned glass filled with ice cubes and garnish with the basil sprig.

Cuzco

1/2 OZ. FRESH LEMON JUICE
1/2 OZ. FRESH GRAPEFRUIT JUICE
3/4 OZ. SIMPLE SYRUP
3/4 OZ. APEROL
2 OZ. PISCO
KIRSCHWASSER
GARNISH: GRAPEFRUIT TWIST

Combine the first five ingredients in a cocktail shaker, add ice cubes, cover, and shake thoroughly. Strain into a Kirschwasser-rinsed highball glass filled with ice cubes and garnish with the grapefruit twist.

Doctor Funk No. 2

¾ OZ. FRESH LIME JUICE

1 DASH OF ABSINTHE

1 DASH OF ANGOSTURA BITTERS

½ OZ. FALERNUM

½ OZ. GRENADINE

1½ OZ. DARK RUM

SODA WATER

GARNISH: LIME WEDGE

Combine the first six ingredients in a cocktail shaker, add ice cubes, cover, and shake thoroughly. Strain into a hurricane glass filled with ice, top with soda water, and garnish with the lime wedge.

East India Cocktail No. 1

¼ OZ. FRESH PINEAPPLE JUICE

1 DASH OF ANGOSTURA BITTERS

¼ OZ. TRIPLE SEC

½ OZ. JAMAICA RUM

1½ OZ. BRANDY

GARNISHES: LEMON TWIST, MARASCHINO CHERRY

Combine all of the ingredients in a cocktail shaker, add ice cubes, cover, and shake thoroughly. Strain into a chilled cocktail glass and garnish with the lemon twist and cherry.

El Manguita

5 FRESH MANGO CHUNKS

1/2 OZ. SIMPLE SYRUP

3/4 OZ. FRESH LIME JUICE

1 PINCH OF GROUND CHILE

2 OZ. WHITE RUM

GARNISH: LIME WHEEL

In a mixing glass muddle the mango chunks with the simple syrup. Add the rest of the ingredients, top with ice cubes, cover, and shake thoroughly. Strain into a chilled cocktail glass and garnish with the lime wheel.

tradesecret

The right glassware and garnishes can transform a tropical cocktail party into an island getaway. Oftentimes, devotees ask their guests to dress the part. Vintage tiki glasses and reproductions can be found affordably online. While most drinks require little in the way of garnish, tropical cocktails are improved by whimsical garnishes such as umbrellas, swizzles, and various spent fruit shells that can be filled with overproof rum and set on fire. This is a category of drinks where you're expected to have fun with themes and not take things too seriously.

Hai Karate

1 OZ. FRESH LIME JUICE

1 OZ. FRESH PINEAPPLE JUICE

1 OZ. FRESH ORANGE JUICE

1 DASH OF ANGOSTURA BITTERS

1 TSP. MAPLE SYRUP

2 OZ. AGED RUM

GARNISHES: MARASCHINO CHERRY, ORANGE WHEEL

Combine all of the ingredients in a cocktail shaker, add ice cubes, cover, and shake thoroughly. Strain into a Collins glass filled with ice cubes and garnish with the cherry skewered into the orange wheel.

Hotel Nacionál

1 OZ. FRESH PINEAPPLE JUICE

½ OZ. FRESH LIME JUICE

½ OZ. SIMPLE SYRUP

¼ OZ. APRICOT BRANDY

2 OZ. AGED RUM

GARNISH: EDIBLE ORCHID

Combine all of the ingredients in a cocktail shaker, add ice cubes, cover, and shake thoroughly. Strain into a chilled cocktail glass and garnish with the edible orchid.

Hai Karate

Mayan Summer

1 ORANGE WHEEL

½ OZ. DEMERARA SYRUP (SIMPLE SYRUP MADE WITH DEMERARA SUGAR)

¼ OZ. FRESH LEMON JUICE

1 PINCH OF GROUND CINNAMON

1 DASH OF ANGOSTURA BITTERS

2 OZ. AGED RUM

GARNISH: CINNAMON STICK

In a mixing glass muddle the orange wheel with the Demerara syrup. Add the rest of the ingredients, top with ice cubes, cover, and shake thoroughly. Strain into an old-fashioned glass filled with ice cubes and garnish with the cinnamon stick.

Nuestra Paloma

1 OZ. FRESH LIME JUICE

½ OZ. FRESH GRAPEFRUIT JUICE

2 DASHES OF ANGOSTURA BITTERS

¾ OZ. TRIPLE SEC

½ OZ. ELDERFLOWER LIQUEUR

2 OZ. BLANCO TEQUILA

GARNISH: GRAPEFRUIT HALF-WHEEL

Combine all of the ingredients in a cocktail shaker, add ice cubes, cover, and shake thoroughly. Strain into a Collins glass filled with ice cubes and garnish with the grapefruit half-wheel inside the rim of the glass.

Piña Agave

2 1/2" CUCUMBER SLICES, PLUS 1 FOR GARNISH

1 OZ. FRESH PINEAPPLE JUICE

3/4 OZ. FRESH LEMON JUICE

1/2 OZ. AGAVE NECTAR

1 1/2 OZ. BLANCO TEQUILA

LEMON-LIME SODA

In a mixing glass muddle 2 cucumber slices. Add the next four ingredients, top with ice cubes, cover, and shake thoroughly. Strain into a chilled cocktail glass, top with soda, and garnish with the remaining cucumber slice.

Queens Road Cocktail

1/2 OZ. FRESH LIME JUICE

1/2 OZ. FRESH ORANGE JUICE

1/2 OZ. HONEY SYRUP (SEE PAGE 36)

1/4 OZ. GINGER LIQUEUR

1 1/2 OZ. WHITE RUM

Combine all of the ingredients in a cocktail shaker, add ice cubes, cover, and shake thoroughly. Strain into an old-fashioned glass filled with ice cubes.

Restless Native

1½ OZ. FRESH LIME JUICE

¾ OZ. WHITE CRÈME DE CACAO

2 OZ. COCONUT RUM

GARNISH: SPIRAL-CUT LENGTH OF LIME PEEL

Combine all of the ingredients in a cocktail shaker, add ice cubes, cover, and shake thoroughly. Strain into a chilled cocktail glass and garnish with the lime peel.

The Rio Fix

¾ OZ. FRESH LIME JUICE

½ OZ. FRESH PINEAPPLE JUICE

½ OZ. MARASCHINO LIQUEUR

1½ OZ. CACHAÇA

PASTIS

Combine the first four ingredients in a cocktail shaker, add ice cubes, cover, and shake thoroughly. Strain into a pastis-rinsed Champagne flute.

Singapore Sling

Royal Bermuda Yacht Club Cocktail

¾ OZ. FRESH LIME JUICE

½ OZ. FALERNUM

½ OZ. TRIPLE SEC

2 OZ. AGED RUM

GARNISH: LIME WHEEL

Combine all of the ingredients in a cocktail shaker, add ice cubes, cover, and shake thoroughly. Strain into a chilled cocktail glass and garnish with the lime wheel.

Singapore Sling

3 OZ. FRESH PINEAPPLE JUICE

½ OZ. FRESH LIME JUICE

1 DASH OF ANGOSTURA BITTERS

⅓ OZ. GRENADINE

½ OZ. CHERRY BRANDY

¼ OZ. COINTREAU

¼ OZ. BÉNÉDICTINE

1½ OZ. GIN

GARNISHES: MARASCHINO CHERRY, FRESH PINEAPPLE SLICE

Combine all of the ingredients in a cocktail shaker, add ice cubes, cover, and shake thoroughly. Strain into a Collins glass filled with ice cubes and garnish with the maraschino cherry and pineapple slice.

Street & Flynn Special

1/2 OZ. FRESH LIME JUICE

1/2 OZ. ALLSPICE LIQUEUR

1/2 OZ. GINGER LIQUEUR

1 1/2 OZ. DARK RUM

SODA WATER

Combine the first four ingredients in a cocktail shaker, add ice cubes, cover, and shake thoroughly. Strain into a highball glass filled with ice cubes and top with soda water.

tradesecret

Tropical cocktails tend to have a bad reputation for being too sweet. Spending the extra cash on a juicer to prepare fresh pineapple juice or purchasing the most naturally prepared purées on the market will dramatically improve these drinks. The quality of the spirits you use to mix these drinks will also bolster your odds; skimping on low-quality liqueurs is one of the surest pitfalls. The good news is that rum is one of the last spirit categories filled with values, so rev up your blenders!

Tequila Massage

3 ½" CUCUMBER SLICES, PLUS 1 FOR GARNISH

¾ OZ. HONEY SYRUP (SEE PAGE 36)

½ OZ. FRESH LIME JUICE

½ OZ. FRESH GRAPEFRUIT JUICE

2 OZ. BLANCO TEQUILA

In a mixing glass muddle 3 cucumber slices with the honey syrup. Add the rest of the remaining ingredients, top with ice cubes, cover, and shake thoroughly. Strain into an old-fashioned glass filled with ice cubes and garnish with the remaining cucumber slice.

The Tura Kill! Kill!

¾ OZ. FRESH LEMON JUICE

1 OZ. FRESH PINEAPPLE JUICE

½ OZ. FRESH ORANGE JUICE

½ OZ. PASSION FRUIT JUICE

1 DASH OF ANGOSTURA BITTERS

¾ OZ. HONEY SYRUP (SEE PAGE 36)

½ OZ. AGED OVERPROOF RUM

1 OZ. BOURBON WHISKEY

SODA WATER

GARNISH: LIME WHEEL

Pour the first eight ingredients into a blender with about 1 cup of ice cubes and pulse-blend for 10 to 15 seconds. Pour contents into a hurricane glass, top with soda water, and garnish with the lime wheel.

Punch
IT UP

The origin of punch makes for great discourse and debate while standing around the proverbial punch bowl. Regardless of whether it takes its name from the Hindustani panch, which means "five" and is purported to be the number of ingredients needed to make one, or is derived from puncheon, an old English wine cask that, once cut open, made one heck of a big punch bowl, the common denominator is that it's a delicious concoction served in large quantities to make many people happy simultaneously.

In all seriousness, there is no single better drink idea for a host to consider when he or she intends to enjoy the guests' company without the demanding distraction of playing bartender. As for what constitutes a proper punch, the sky's the limit. Any cocktail recipe can be multiplied to fit in a punch bowl, but the essential key for any cold punch is ice, a very big block of it or a handmade mold. Unless otherwise stated, these recipes make approximately twelve 4- to 5-ounce servings.

Agricole Rum Punch

12 OZ. FRESH LIME JUICE

24 DASHES (4 TSP.) OF ANGOSTURA BITTERS

12 OZ. SIMPLE SYRUP

3 OZ. ALLSPICE LIQUEUR

ONE 750-ML BOTTLE AGED RHUM AGRICOLE

GARNISH: FRESHLY GRATED NUTMEG

In a large glass pitcher combine all of the ingredients, top with ice cubes, and stir thoroughly. Strain into a punch bowl and add a large block of ice. Serve in chilled punch cups and garnish each with grated nutmeg.

Amazonian Love Honey

4 OZ. FRESH LEMON JUICE

4 OZ. FRESH ORANGE JUICE

12 DASHES (2 TSP.) OF ORANGE BITTERS

4 OZ. HONEY SYRUP (SEE PAGE 36)

12 OZ. CACHAÇA

ONE 375-ML HALF-BOTTLE CHAMPAGNE, CHILLED

GARNISH: ORANGE TWISTS

In a large glass pitcher combine the first five ingredients, top with ice cubes, and stir thoroughly. Strain into a punch bowl, add a large block of ice, and top with the Champagne. Serve in wine glasses and garnish each with an orange twist.

Amazonian Love Honey

Backyard Blackberry Margarita

Back Porch Swizzle

12 OZ. FRESH PINEAPPLE JUICE

6 OZ. DRY VERMOUTH

6 OZ. GREEN CHARTREUSE

18 OZ. BOURBON WHISKEY

ONE 12-OZ. BOTTLE GINGER BEER, CHILLED

GARNISH: MINT SPRIGS

In a large glass pitcher combine the first four ingredients, top with ice cubes, and stir thoroughly. Strain into a punch bowl, add a large block of ice, and top with the ginger beer. Serve in highball glasses filled with crushed ice and garnish each with a mint sprig.

Backyard Blackberry Margarita

1 PINT FRESH BLACKBERRIES

9 OZ. SIMPLE SYRUP, CHILLED

9 OZ. FRESH LIME JUICE, CHILLED

3 OZ. TRIPLE SEC, CHILLED

18 OZ. BLANCO TEQUILA, CHILLED

ONE 375-ML HALF-BOTTLE CHAMPAGNE, CHILLED

GARNISH: THYME SPRIGS

In a large glass pitcher muddle the blackberries with the simple syrup. Add the next three ingredients, stir, and strain through a fine-mesh sieve into a punch bowl. Add a large block of ice and top with the Champagne. Serve in wine glasses filled with ice cubes and garnish each with a thyme sprig.

Black Rose

1 PINT FRESH BLACKBERRIES, PLUS 12 EXTRA FOR GARNISH

5 OZ. SIMPLE SYRUP

6 OZ. FRESH LIME JUICE

9 OZ. VODKA

ONE 750-ML BOTTLE DRY ROSÉ WINE

GARNISH: LIME WHEELS

In a large glass pitcher muddle the blackberries with the simple syrup. Add the remaining ingredients, top with ice cubes, and stir thoroughly. Strain through a fine-mesh sieve into a punch bowl and add a large block of ice. Serve in wine glasses filled with ice cubes and garnish each with a lime wheel and a blackberry.

Bloody Mary

EIGHT 6-OZ. CANS OR ONE 46-OZ. CAN TOMATO JUICE

3 OZ. FRESH LEMON JUICE

4 TBSP. WORCESTERSHIRE SAUCE

2 OZ. TABASCO SAUCE

1 TSP. KOSHER SALT

1 TSP. GROUND BLACK PEPPER

1 TSP. CELERY SALT

1 TSP. PREPARED HORSERADISH

18 OZ. VODKA

GARNISH: CELERY STICKS

In a large glass pitcher combine all of the ingredients, top with ice cubes, and stir thoroughly. Strain into a punch bowl and add a large block of ice. Serve in highball glasses filled with ice cubes and garnish each with a celery stick.

Bloody Mary

Bombay Punch

4 OZ. FRESH LEMON JUICE

2 OZ. SIMPLE SYRUP

1 OZ. MARASCHINO LIQUEUR

1 OZ. TRIPLE SEC

8 OZ. COGNAC

8 OZ. AMONTILLADO SHERRY

ONE 750-ML BOTTLE CHAMPAGNE, CHILLED

GARNISH: ASSORTMENT OF WHOLE OR CUT SEASONAL FRUITS

In a large glass pitcher combine the first six ingredients, top with ice cubes, and stir thoroughly. Strain into a punch bowl, add a large block of ice, and top with the Champagne. Serve in chilled punch glasses, garnished with seasonal fruits.

Brahman

20 FRESH BASIL LEAVES, PLUS 12 MORE FOR GARNISH

6 OZ. ORGEAT

12 OZ. FRESH PINEAPPLE JUICE

12 OZ. APPLE JUICE

ONE 750-ML BOTTLE BLENDED SCOTCH WHISKY

In a large glass pitcher muddle 20 basil leaves with the orgeat. Add the rest of the ingredients, top with ice cubes, and stir thoroughly. Strain through a fine-mesh sieve into a punch bowl and add a large block of ice. Serve in highball glasses filled with crushed ice and garnish each with a basil leaf.

Fizzy Lifter

9 OZ. FRESH PINEAPPLE JUICE

6 OZ. FRESH ORANGE JUICE

24 DASHES (4 TSP.) OF ORANGE BITTERS

9 OZ. ELDERFLOWER LIQUEUR

18 OZ. GIN

ONE 375-ML HALF-BOTTLE PROSECCO, CHILLED

GARNISH: ORANGE TWISTS

In a large glass pitcher combine the first five ingredients, top with ice cubes, and stir thoroughly. Strain into a punch bowl, add a large block of ice, and top with the prosecco. Serve in wine glasses and garnish each with an orange twist.

The Horseshoe Sling

8 OZ. FRESH LIME JUICE

4 OZ. FRESH PINEAPPLE JUICE

24 DASHES (4 TSP.) OF ANGOSTURA BITTERS

3 OZ. BÉNÉDICTINE

3 OZ. CHERRY BRANDY

6 OZ. TRIPLE SEC

ONE 750-ML BOTTLE BLANCO TEQUILA

12 OZ. SODA WATER

GARNISH: ORANGE WHEELS

In a large glass pitcher combine the first seven ingredients, top with ice cubes, and stir thoroughly. Strain into a punch bowl, add a large block of ice, and top with the soda water. Serve in wine glasses filled with ice cubes and garnish each with an orange wheel.

Lime Bumboo

8 OZ. FRESH LIME JUICE

6 OZ. DEMERARA SYRUP (SIMPLE SYRUP MADE WITH DEMERARA SUGAR)

3 OZ. TRIPLE SEC

ONE 750-ML BOTTLE AGED RUM

GARNISHES: FRESHLY GRATED NUTMEG, LIME WHEELS

In a large glass pitcher combine all of the ingredients, top with ice cubes, and stir thoroughly. Strain into a punch bowl and add a large block of ice. Serve in chilled punch cups and garnish each with grated nutmeg and a lime wheel.

tradesecret

When it's hot outside, we tend to dehydrate quickly, which can exacerbate the effects of a cocktail on your constitution. Always make water available and accessible whenever you're serving mixed drinks. Leaving out plenty of cups and pitchers of water or coolers filled with mini bottles that can be easily consumed will encourage your guests to stay properly hydrated.

Lime Bumboo

Main Line Wine

12 OZ. FRESH LEMON JUICE

12 OZ. SIMPLE SYRUP

3 OZ. YELLOW CHARTREUSE

6 DASHES OF ORANGE BITTERS

1 OZ. GRAND MARNIER

1 375-ML BOTTLE CABERNET

16 OZ. AGED RUM

GARNISH: ORANGE HALF-WHEELS

Add everything to a punch bowl with a large block of ice. Serve in teacups filled with crushed ice and garnish each with an orange half-wheel.

Max's Mistake

12 OZ. PASSION FRUIT NECTAR

12 OZ. FRESH LEMON JUICE

24 DASHES (4 TSP.) OF ANGOSTURA BITTERS

¾ OZ. HONEY SYRUP (SEE PAGE 36)

ONE 750-ML BOTTLE GIN

TWO 7-OZ. BOTTLES FEVER TREE BITTER LEMON SODA, CHILLED

Working in three batches, combine the first five ingredients in a blender. Top each batch with 4 cups of crushed ice and pulse-blend for 10 seconds. Pour into wine glasses and top each serving with 1 oz. of bitter lemon soda.

Old Navy Punch

5 OZ. FRESH LEMON JUICE

2 OZ. FRESH ORANGE JUICE

2 OZ. SIMPLE SYRUP

8 OZ. AGED OVERPROOF RUM

5 OZ. COGNAC

1 OZ. PEACH BRANDY

ONE 375-ML HALF-BOTTLE CHAMPAGNE, CHILLED

GARNISH: FRESHLY GRATED NUTMEG

In a large glass pitcher combine the first six ingredients, top with ice cubes, and stir thoroughly. Strain into a punch bowl, add a large block of ice, and top with the Champagne. Serve in chilled punch cups and garnish with grated nutmeg.

Pearl Button

6 OZ. FRESH LIME JUICE

8 OZ. LILLET BLANC

ONE 750-ML BOTTLE CACHAÇA

THREE 6-OZ. BOTTLES PELLEGRINO LIMONATA, CHILLED

GARNISH: 12 GRAPEFRUIT HALF-WHEELS

In a large glass pitcher combine the first three ingredients, top with ice cubes, and stir thoroughly. Strain into a punch bowl, add a large block of ice, and top with the bitter lemon soda. Serve in wine glasses filled with ice cubes and garnish each with a grapefruit half-wheel inside the rim of the glass.

Rangoon Gin Cobbler

Rangoon Gin Cobbler

12 OZ. FRESH LIME JUICE

6 OZ. FRESH GRAPEFRUIT JUICE

24 DASHES (4 TSP.) OF ANGOSTURA BITTERS

6 OZ. AGAVE NECTAR

8 OZ. TRIPLE SEC

ONE 750-ML BOTTLE GIN

GARNISH: FRESHLY GRATED ORANGE ZEST

In a large glass pitcher combine all of the ingredients, top with ice cubes, and stir thoroughly. Strain into a punch bowl and add a large block of ice. Serve in punch cups filled with crushed ice and garnish with grated orange zest.

Sangria

1 THINLY SLICED ORANGE

1 THINLY SLICED LIME

4 OZ. SIMPLE SYRUP

8 OZ. BRANDY

4 OZ. TRIPLE SEC

ONE 750-ML BOTTLE RED WINE

12 OZ. SODA WATER, CHILLED

GARNISH: ASSORTMENT OF WHOLE OR CUT SEASONAL FRUITS

In a large glass pitcher combine the first six ingredients, cover, and store in the refrigerator overnight. Strain into a punch bowl, add a large block of ice, and top with the soda water. Serve in wine glasses filled with ice cubes and garnish each with assorted seasonal fruits.

Southern Peach

6 OZ. PEACH PURÉE

6 OZ. FRESH LEMON JUICE

4 OZ. SIMPLE SYRUP

12 OZ. BOURBON WHISKEY

ONE 375-ML HALF-BOTTLE CHAMPAGNE, CHILLED

GARNISH: FRESH PEACH SLICES

In a large glass pitcher combine the first four ingredients, top with ice cubes, and stir thoroughly. Strain into a punch bowl, add a large block of ice, and top with the Champagne. Serve in wine glasses and garnish each with a peach slice.

Summer Shack

12 DASHES (2 TSP.) OF ORANGE BITTERS

8 OZ. GIN

8 OZ. LILLET BLANC

4 OZ. ELDERFLOWER LIQUEUR

ONE 750-ML BOTTLE SAUVIGNON BLANC

GARNISH: LEMON TWISTS

In a large glass pitcher combine all of the ingredients, top with ice cubes, and stir thoroughly. Strain into a punch bowl and add a large block of ice. Serve in wine glasses and garnish each with a lemon twist.

tradesecret

Always look over the guest list before deciding on what drinks to serve. Spirit preferences, allergies, or dietary constraints can make or break a cocktail hour. You can't make everyone happy, but taking the time to inquire what people prefer will make your guests feel special regardless of what you choose. When serving classics, doing a little research about the origins of the recipes or the production processes behind the spirits used to mix them may come in handy and impress your guests. Google is a great place to start.

Tropical White Sangria

2 VERY RIPE MANGOES, PEELED, PITTED, AND CUT INTO 1" CUBES

4 STALKS LEMONGRASS, WHITE STALK ONLY, CHOPPED INTO 1" SLICES

6 FRESH LYCHEES, PEELED, SPLIT, AND PITTED

3 OZ. COGNAC

1 1/2 OZ. AMARETTO

1 1/2 OZ. TRIPLE SEC

TWO 750-ML BOTTLES PINOT BLANC

GARNISH: 1 PINT FRESH RASPBERRIES

In a large glass pitcher combine all the ingredients, cover, and store in the refrigerator overnight. Strain into a punch bowl and add a large block of ice. Serve in wine glasses filled with ice cubes and garnish each with fresh raspberries.

MEASURES

Here are conversions for unusual measures typically found in nineteenth-century recipes:

Pony/Cordial = 1 ounce

Pousse Café Glass = 1½ ounces

Cocktail Glass = 2 ounces

Gill = 4 ounces

Wine Glass = 4 ounces

Small Tumbler = 8 ounces

Large Tumbler = 16 ounces

STANDARD BAR MEASUREMENTS (U.S.)

Pony = 1 ounce

1 ounce = 3 centiliters

Jigger, shot = 1½ ounces

Mixing Glass = 16 ounces

Splash = ½ ounce

Dash = 6 drops = ⅙ teaspoon

OTHER MEASURES

6 drops = 1 dash

6 dashes = 1 teaspoon

1 teaspoon = $\frac{1}{6}$ ounce

2 teaspoons = $\frac{1}{3}$ ounce

1 tablespoon = $\frac{1}{2}$ ounce

2 tablespoons = 1 ounce

$\frac{1}{4}$ cup = 2 ounces

$\frac{1}{2}$ cup = 4 ounces

1 cup or $\frac{1}{2}$ pint = 8 ounces

2 cups or 1 pint = 16 ounces

4 cups, 2 pints, or 1 quart = 32 ounces

BOTTLE SIZE MEASURES

Split = 187 ml = 6.4 ounces

Half-Bottle = 375 ml = 12.7 ounces

Fifth or Bottle = 750 ml = 25.4 ounces

Liter = 1000 ml = 33.8 ounces

Magnum = 1.5 liters = 2 wine bottles

Jeroboam = 3 liters = 4 wine bottles

Rehoboam = 6 wine bottles

Methuselah = 8 wine bottles

Salmanazar = 12 wine bottles

Balthazar = 16 wine bottles

Nebuchadnezzar = 20 wine bottles

Sovereign = 34 wine bottles

index